Helping Animals

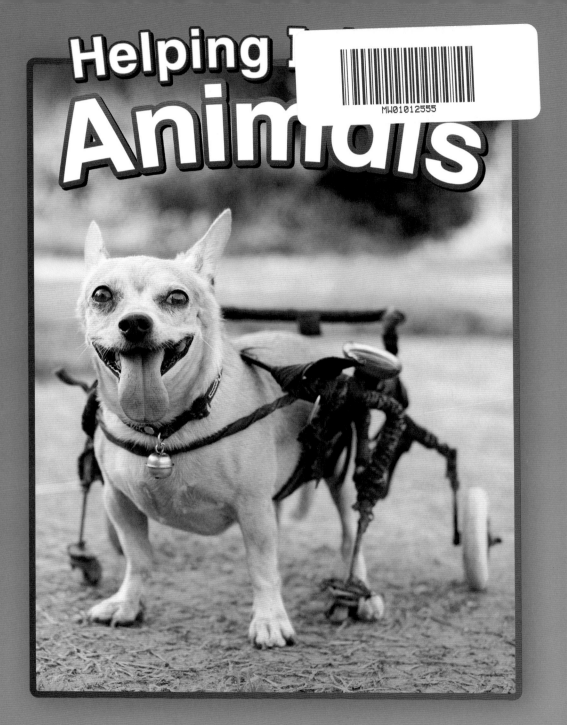

Anne Montgomery

 Smithsonian

Consultants

Jen Zoon
Communications Specialist
Office of Communications
Smithsonian National Zoo

Amy Zoque
STEM Coordinator and Instructional Coach
Vineyard STEM School
Ontario Montclair School District

Publishing Credits

Rachelle Cracchiolo, M.S.Ed., *Publisher*

Conni Medina, M.A.Ed., *Editor in Chief*

Diana Kenney, M.A.Ed., NBCT, *Series Developer*

Emily R. Smith, M.A.Ed., *Content Director*

Véronique Bos, *Creative Director*

Robin Erickson, *Art Director*

Michelle Jovin, M.A., *Associate Editor*

Mindy Duits, *Series Designer*

Lee Aucoin, *Senior Graphic Designer*

Smithsonian Science Education Center

Image Credits: pp.2–3 USFWS Photo/Alamy; pp.4–8, p.10 © Smithsonian; p.11 (right) Shahjehan/Shutterstock; pp.12–13 Courtesy 3D Systems; pp.14–15 Shawn Rocco/MCT/Newscom; p.16 Pascal Deloche/Godong/ picture-alliance/Newscom; p.17 Paula Bronstein/Getty Images; p.18 ZJAN/ markstevensp/Newscom; p.19 (top) Jim Damaske/Zuma Press/Newscom; p.19 (bottom) Barry Bland/Barcroft Media/Getty Images; all other images from iStock and/or Shutterstock.

Library of Congress Cataloging-in-Publication Data

Names: Rice, Dona, author.
Title: Helping injured animals / Dona Herweck Rice, Smithsonian.
Description: Huntington Beach, CA : Teacher Created Materials, [2020] |
   Audience: K to Grade 3. |
Identifiers: LCCN 2018051873 (print) | LCCN 2018054251 (ebook) | ISBN
   9781493868865 (eBook) | ISBN 9781493866465 (paperback)
Subjects: LCSH: Veterinary surgery--Technological innovation--Juvenile
   literature. | Prosthesis--Juvenile literature. | Three-dimensional imaging
   in medicine--Juvenile literature.
Classification: LCC SF911 (ebook) | LCC SF911 .R53 2020 (print) | DDC
   636.089/7--dc23
LC record available at https://lccn.loc.gov/2018051873

Teacher Created Materials

5301 Oceanus Drive
Huntington Beach, CA 92649-1030
www.tcmpub.com
ISBN 978-1-4938-6646-5
© 2019 Teacher Created Materials, Inc.
Printed in China
51497

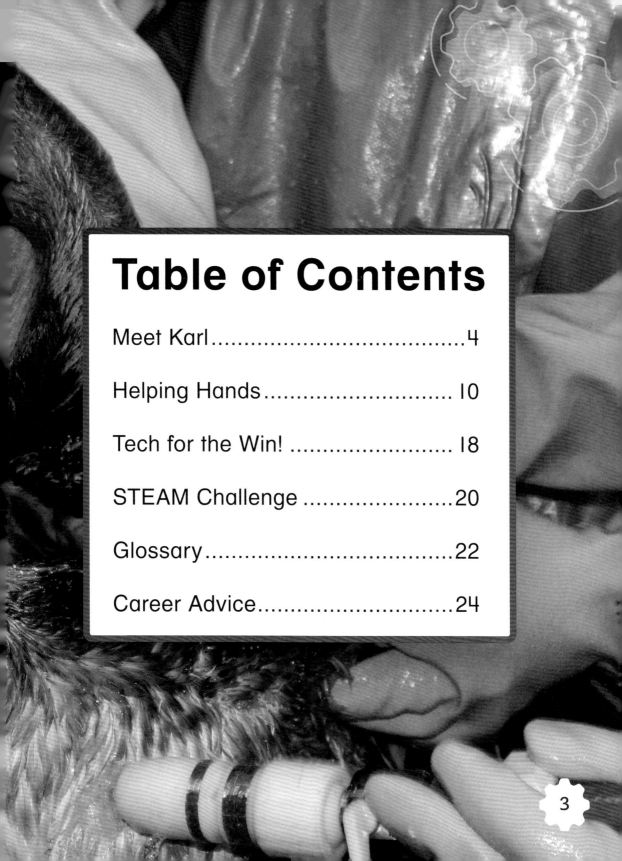

Table of Contents

Meet Karl

Karl is a hornbill who looks just like his name sounds. His **bill** looks like a long horn. Karl uses his bill to pick up food. It would be very hard for Karl to eat without it.

Karl the hornbill

Karl uses his bill to hold food.

Sadly, the lower part of Karl's bill had worn away! Scientists helped him. They used a **3-D printer**. With it, they made a new part. The part is called a *prosthetic beak*.

Karl's bill has worn away.

How do you say that?
prosthetic = (praws-THEH-tik)

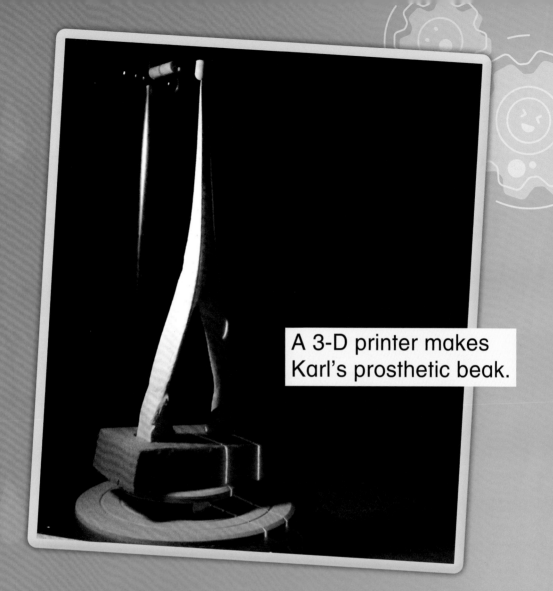

A 3-D printer makes Karl's prosthetic beak.

Animal Avengers

This group of people helps animals. They give their time and talents. They raise money as well. They help solve problems and protect animals.

The new part of Karl's bill is just right for him. Now he can use his bill like any other bird.

Technology is amazing. So is Karl!

Doctors make sure Karl's new beak will fit.

Who Are You?

Some animals use color to help spot friends and foes. Some toucans' beaks are orange. Prosthetic beaks for these birds must be orange as well. If not, the birds will be **rejected**!

Helping Hands

Karl is not the only one to get help. Prosthetic parts are made for many animals. The new parts may not work the same as those made by nature. But they help.

Karl with his prosthetic beak

This runner's prosthetic leg is based on a cheetah's leg.

Helping People

Prosthetic parts are made for people too. They can replace missing or hurt body parts. They help people move and live in new ways.

Derby was born with badly formed front legs. He could not run at all. Scientists found a way to help. They gave Derby prosthetic legs. Now Derby can run with his prosthetic legs.

Derby runs with his prosthetic legs.

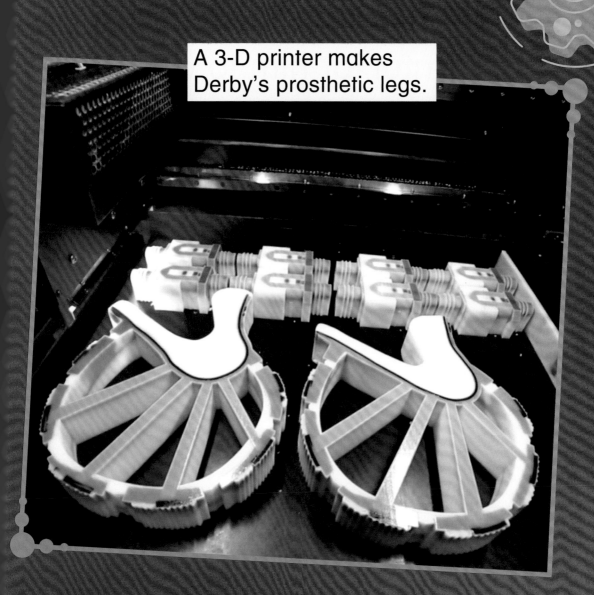

A 3-D printer makes Derby's prosthetic legs.

Cyrano was very sick. Doctors helped him feel better. But one knee was left too weak and painful for him to walk.

Doctors made a new knee for him. Once again, he could move like any other cat!

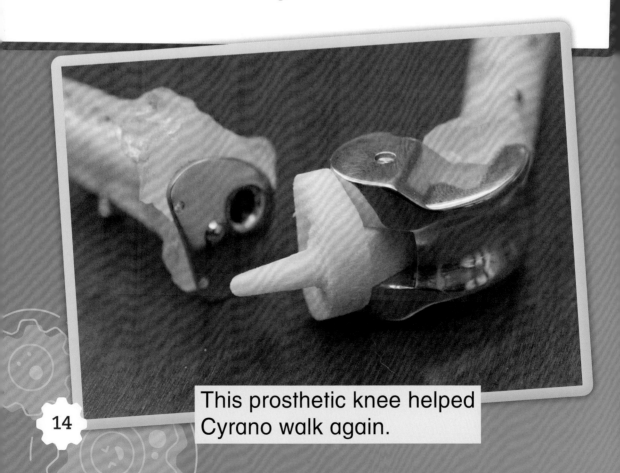

This prosthetic knee helped Cyrano walk again.

Cyrano the tabby cat

Some prosthetic parts are huge! Take Motala the elephant. She hurt her front leg while looking for food one day. She could not walk anymore. Then, a group of people made her a new front leg. Motala could walk again!

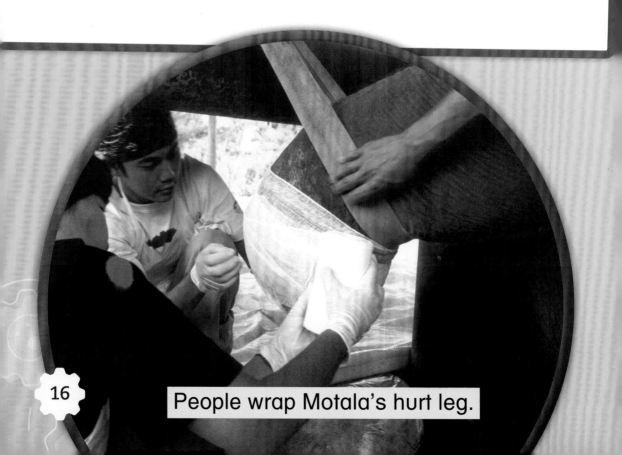

People wrap Motala's hurt leg.

Motala walks on her prosthetic leg.

Tech for the Win!

Prosthetic parts are better than ever. A lot of that is thanks to 3-D printing. It makes light parts that move well. The parts last a long time too. Technology makes it all happen!

This cat has prosthetic back legs.

This dolphin has a prosthetic tail.

This dog has two prosthetic legs.

STEAM CHALLENGE

The Problem

Pip the dog needs your help! She has hurt her tail, which she uses to show her feelings. Now she cannot wag it to show she is happy. She cannot lower it to show she is sad. Pip needs you to make her a tail so she can show what she feels.

The Goals

- Make a model of a tail with any material that can move and bend.
- Make a light and soft tail so it will not hurt Pip.
- Make sure your prosthetic tail can be attached to Pip.

Research and Brainstorm

Why does a dog need to communicate? What other ways can a dog "say" what it feels?

Design and Build

Draw your plan. How will it work? What materials will you use? Build your model!

Test and Improve

Test the prosthetic tail by attaching it to your body. Try to show feelings with it. Does it work? Can you improve it? Try again.

Reflect and Share

Why should people help animals with prosthetic parts? Are there other ways to help animals?

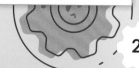

Glossary

3-D printer

bill

rejected

technology

Do you want to help injured animals?
Here are some ideas to get you started.

"If you want to protect our planet and its animals, there are many different careers for you!" — *Dr. Jilian Fazio, Research Fellow, Center for Species Survival*

"I have always loved animals. When I was young, I saw animals in danger. That made me want to make sure nothing like that happened again." — *Chris Crowe, Animal Keeper*